Sock Loom Projects...
More than just socks!

This book includes complete step by step instructions, with lots of photos and charts that make knitting socks super easy. No knitting experience needed!

Make thick cozy socks, or thin elegant socks, your choice! This book features patterns for 2 sock looms and a variety of projects.....socks in all sizes, mittens, leg warmers, and fingerless gloves.

Contents

KB Sock Loom

Fine Gauge Sock Loom Projects

7 patterns using sock weight yarn, for tight knit socks and fingerless gloves.

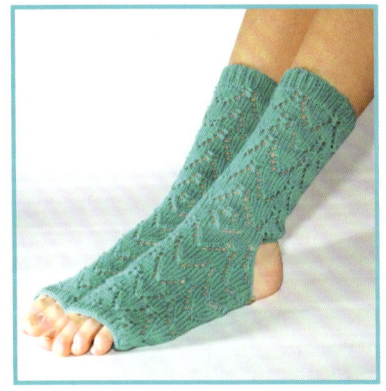

KB Sock Loom ❷

Regular Gauge Sock Loom Projects

7 patterns using worsted weight yarn for thick, cozy socks, legwarmers, and mittens..

MEN'S TUBE SOCKS PAGE 18

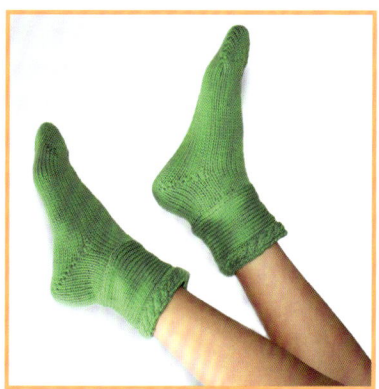

SIDEWAYS PAGE 24

MONKEY PAGE 33

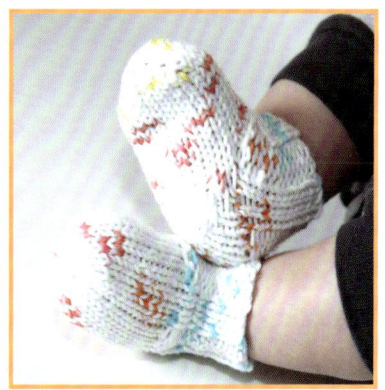

BABY PAGE 36

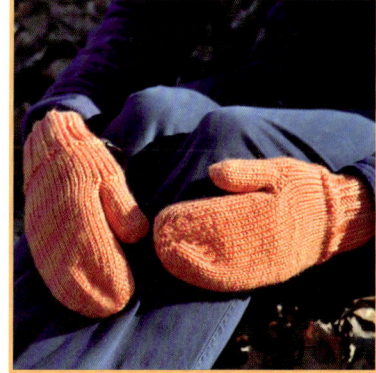

HIS & HER MITTENS PAGE 39

SIMPLE RIB PAGE 45

LEG WARMERS PAGE 55

CABLE WRISTERS PAGE 57

Sock Loom Projects

This book takes you through the basic instructions for knitting socks on sock looms. The 15 projects include socks for children and adults, mittens, fingerless gloves, and legwarmers. The samples featured were made using KB Sock Looms, but any fine gauge and regular gauge loom can be used.

About Yarns...

When choosing your yarn, think about the look, feel and thickness of what you would like to create. Do you want to make a thick sock or footie, or a thinner sock that will fit into all shoes? For thick, warm, and cozy socks, use worsted weight yarn. For thinner socks, use fingering, sport or DK weight sock yarn.

How much yarn will you need for your project? It all depends on what you want to make. This chart shows the average number of yards needed for socks using different thicknesses of yarn.

Suggested Yardage for a Pair of Socks

	Toddler	Child	Women	Men
Fingering	270	320	420	525
Sport	210	250	360	430
DK	200	230	330	400
Worsted	180	200	310	370

Sock Looms

In this book, patterns feature 2 different types of sock looms.
- A fine gauge loom to make thinner, lighter socks and gloves, using a fingering or DK weight sock yarn.
- A regular gauge sock loom to make thicker socks, footies and mittens using a worsted weight yarn.

Reference chart on the following page.

Yarn Weight Symbol & Category Names	SUPER FINE 1 SUPER FIN Super Fino	FINE 2 FIN Fino	LIGHT 3 LEGER Ligero	MEDIUM 4 MOYEN Medio
Type of Yarns in Category	Sock, Fingering, Baby	Sport, Baby	DK, Light Worsted	Worsted, Afghan, Aran
Knit Gauge Range* in Stockinette Stitch to 1 inch	7–8 sts	6–6.5 sts	5–6 st	4-5 sts
Recommended Loom Gauge	FG	FG	FG	RG

FG=Fine Gauge,   RG=Regular Gauge

Fine Gauge Sock Looms

Regular Gauge Loom

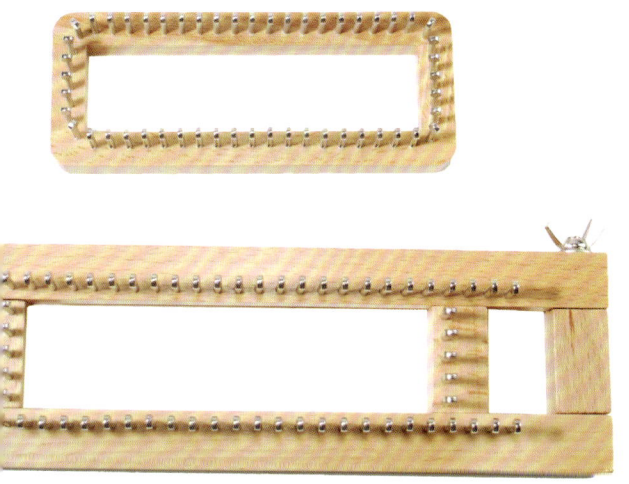

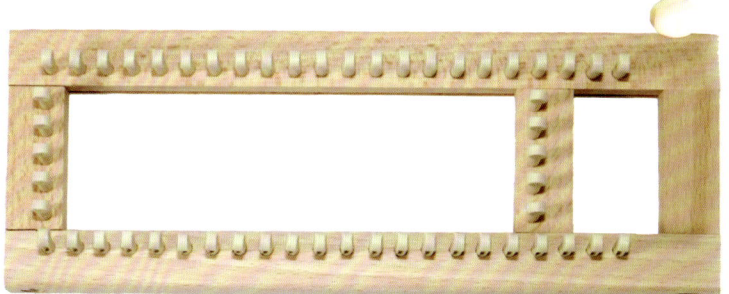

A regular gauge sock loom has larger pegs and greater spacing that will accommodate thicker worsted weight yarn.

Determining number of pegs for your Socks:

First, measure around the ball of your foot at the widest part at base of toes for circumference.

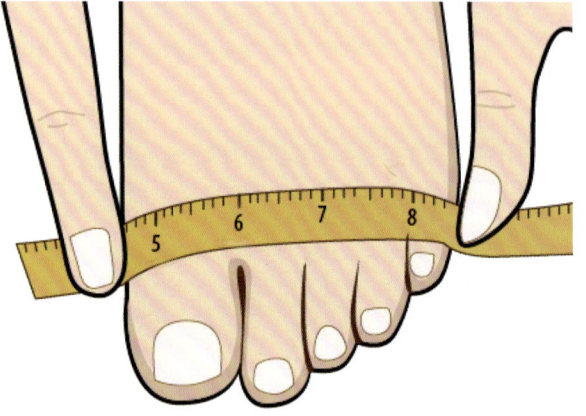

Number of pegs for socks (Averages)

Using a fine gauge sock loom with fingering weight yarn (KB Sock Loom, original)

7" ball of foot measurement = 42, 44 pegs

8" ball of foot measurement = 48, 50 pegs

9" ball of foot measurement = 54, 56 pegs

Using a regular gauge sock loom with worsted weight yarn (KB Sock Loom②, regular gauge)

7" ball of foot measurement = 32 pegs

8" ball of foot measurement = 36 pegs

9" ball of foot measurement = 40 pegs

Then create a sample swatch (a small section of knitting with the yarn and the kind of loom you plan to use for the socks). Once you have created your swatch, determine your gauge. This means, how many stitches are required for 1-inch of knitting in your swatch (use measure tape). This number of stitches = the gauge. Then use chart below to find ideal number of pegs.

Suggested Number of Pegs for Sock (according to gauge)

Gauge(sts per inch)	Foot Ball Circumference	Suggested Number of Pegs
9	6 (7, 8, 9, 10, 11, 12)	48(56, 64, 72, 82, 90, 98)
8	6 (7, 8, 9, 10, 11, 12)	44(50, 58, 64, 72, 80, 86)
7	6 (7, 8, 9, 10, 11, 12)	38(44, 50, 56, 64, 70, 76)
6	6 (7, 8, 9, 10, 11, 12)	32(38, 44, 48, 54, 60, 64)
5	6 (7, 8, 9, 10, 11, 12)	28(32, 36, 40, 46, 50, 54)
4	6 (7, 8, 9, 10, 11, 12)	22(26, 28, 32, 36, 40, 44)
3	6 (7, 8, 9, 10, 11, 12)	16(18, 22, 24, 28, 30, 32)

Note: 7 is the most common fine loom gauge. 5 is the most common regular loom gauge.

To manually calculate pegs required, multiply the circumference number by the gauge number. The resulting number will be multiplied by .88 (-12%) to provide the negative ease required for socks. The resulting number is the number of pegs recommended for your socks. If you get an uneven number, round up to arrive at the correct even number of pegs.

Remember these are approximates, and are based on sock yarn weight and worsted weight sample swatches. Use a larger amount of pegs (2-4) for wide feet or large ankles. Use the ribbing stitch to provide a flexible cuff. You will find your proper sizing very quickly, and can rely on instructions within specific patterns.

Length of Sock:

You also want to determine how high up your leg you want the sock to go: to the ankle? the calf? the knee? The length of sock is based on number of rounds worked. Just remember, the toe adds approximately 2" to the length of the sock, so be sure to measure accordingly when determining foot length.

Gather your tools:
Sock loom
Knit hook
Scissors
Tapestry needle
Measuring tape
Crochet hook

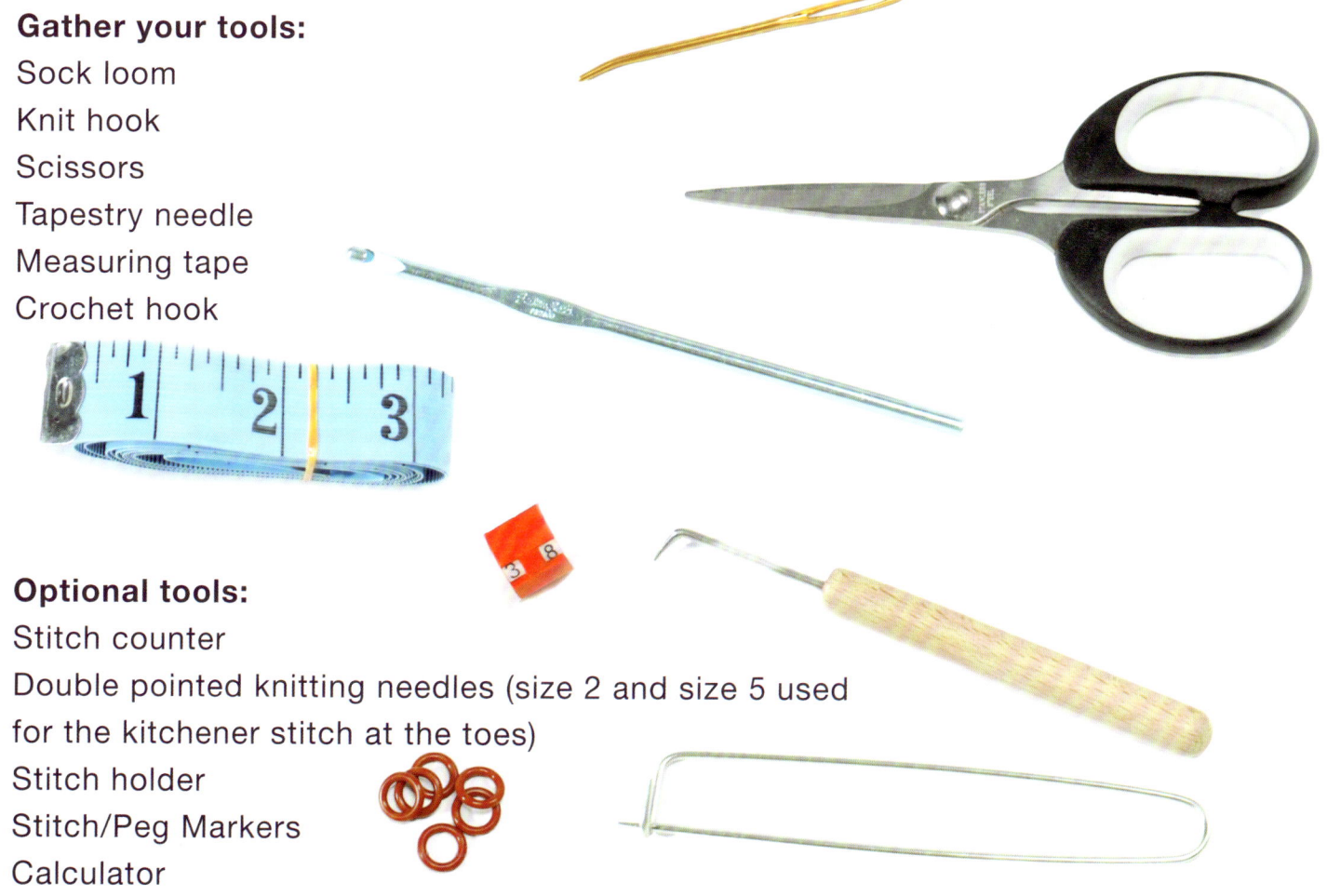

Optional tools:
Stitch counter
Double pointed knitting needles (size 2 and size 5 used for the kitchener stitch at the toes)
Stitch holder
Stitch/Peg Markers
Calculator
Masking tape (for marking sts in weave patterns)

Basic Sock Knitting

Set your sock loom to the correct number of pegs determined above.
To begin your sock, start by casting on the stitches.

E-wrap Cast On: This cast on is recommended for socks. It creates a flexible edge that provides enough give for the heel, and yet stays tight on the leg.

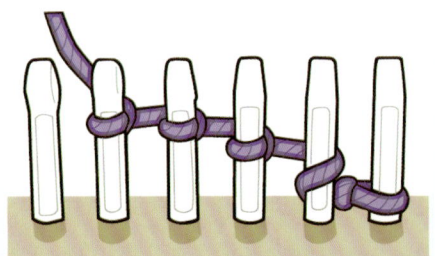 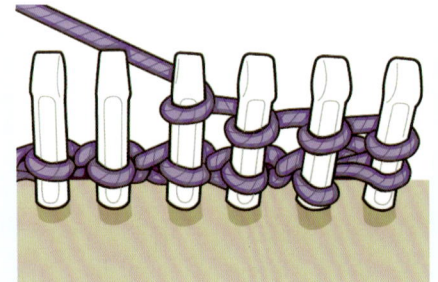 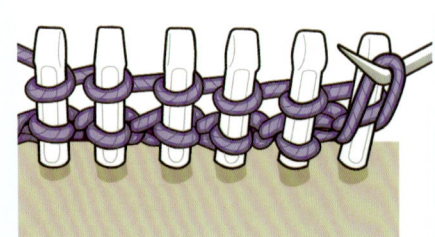

1. Tie a slip knot onto the first peg, and wrap in a clockwise motion around the loom; wrap each peg counterclockwise to end.

2. To finish the cast on, wrap each peg one more time to create two loops on each peg.

3. Work these stitches by lifting the bottom loop over the top (known as Knit Off (KO), leaving one loop on the peg. This is the e-wrap method.

Chain Cast On: This cast on is tighter than the e-wrap cast on and is not recommended for socks, but is great for mittens, fingerless gloves, or leg warmers.

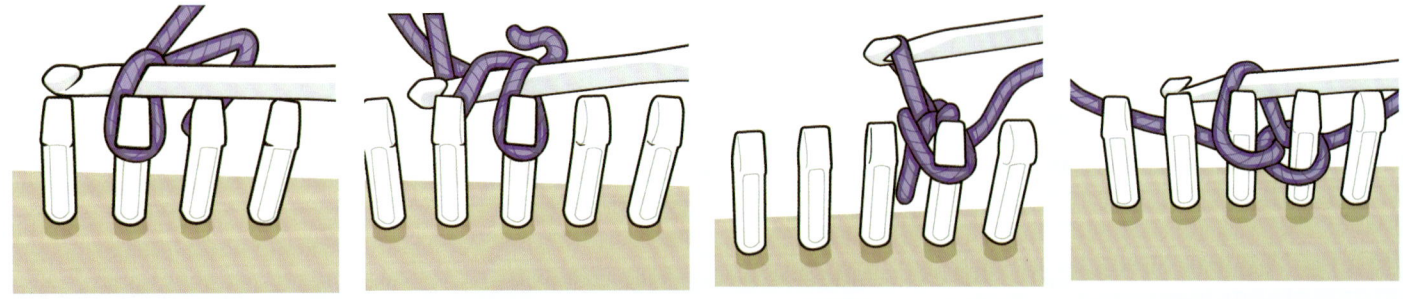

1. Begin with a slip knot on the first peg. Place crochet hook into the slip knot from top of loop.

2. Grab the working yarn. Keep the working yarn to the inside of the loom during the entire cast on.

3. Pull the working yarn through the stitch on the peg. Place this newly formed loop onto 2nd peg.

Then repeat the process on all pegs. Your stitches are now cast on and you are ready to begin your stitches.

Stitches

Knit Stitch (k st): Place working yarn above loops; insert hook below each loop and grab working yarn and pull under loop and lift off peg. Replace the new loop onto peg. This stitch creates the most stretch.

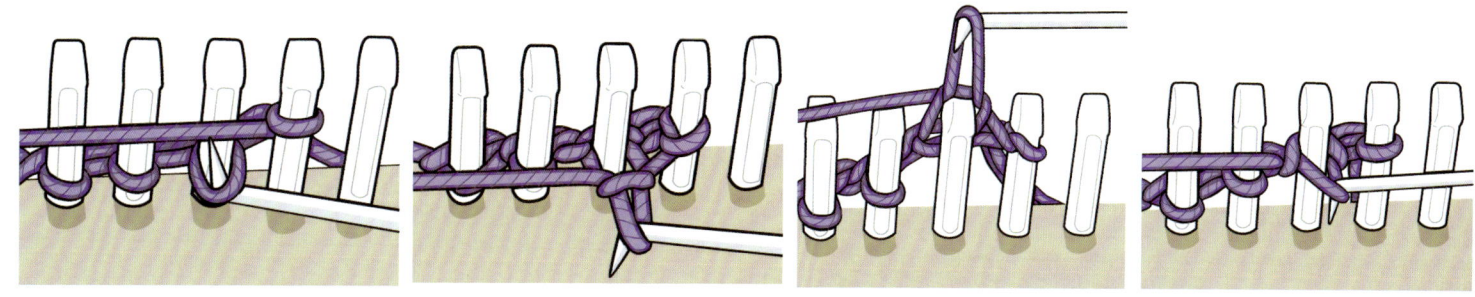

Flat Stitch (f st): Place working yarn above loops on pegs, lift loops off and over pegs. This is the easiest and fastest stitch; it is also a tighter stitch.

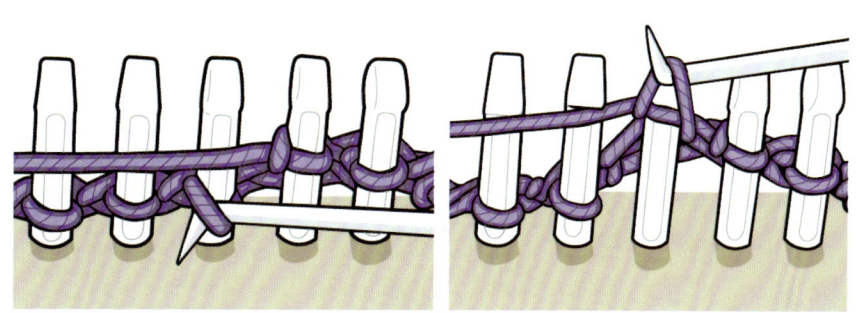

Hint: When using the flat stitch, it is important to make sure that you do not pull the working yarn too tight, only guide it. If you do, the stitches will be very difficult to lift over. Allow plenty of yarn into each stitch before moving on.

U-Stitch (u-st): This stitch looks just like the flat stitch but a bit looser. Wrap the working yarn around the front of the peg and hold toward back of loom, hook bottom stitch over top stitch.

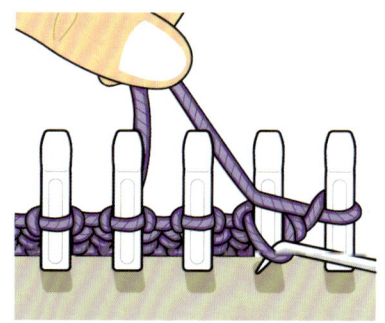

NOTE: The knit stitch, flat stitch and the u-stitch are all stockinette stitches that can be used interchangeably in patterns, but remember if going from a knit stitch to flat stitch, more pegs will need to be added to get the same width of sock.

Purl Stitch (p st): Place working yarn below loop; insert hook from top of loop and grab working yarn and pull under loop and lift off peg. Replace the new loop onto peg. Purl stitch is used alone or with knit stitch to form ribbing for cuff.

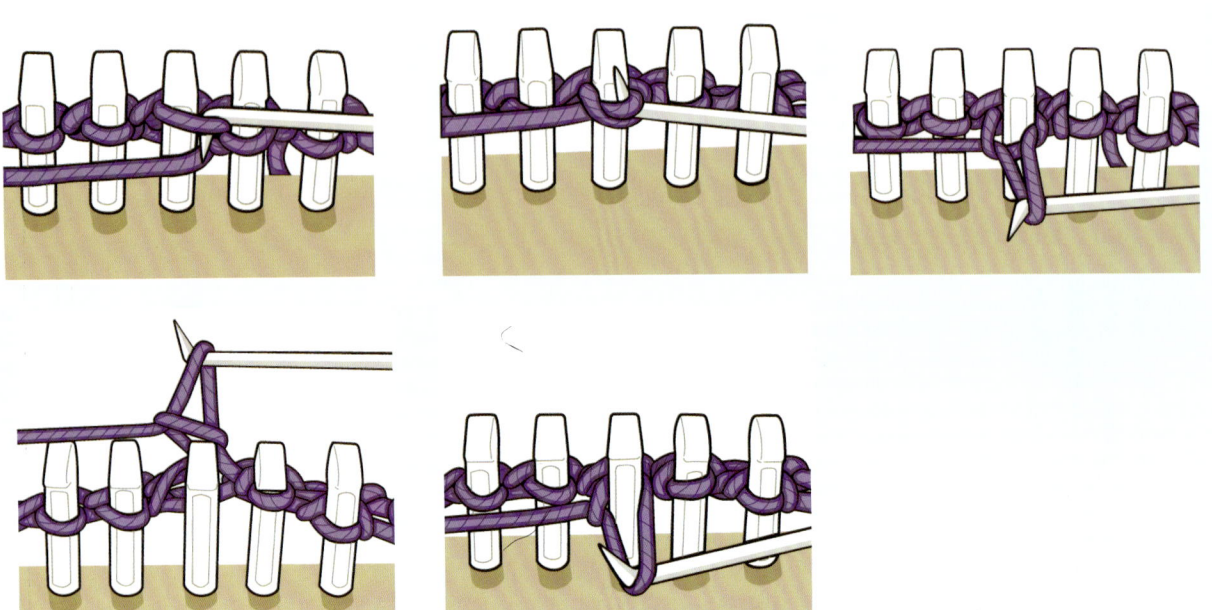

Wrap & Turn: Used to change direction of knitting. Lift loop off of peg and place working yarn around back of peg; replace loop back on to the peg. This will create one loop and one wrapped yarn on peg.

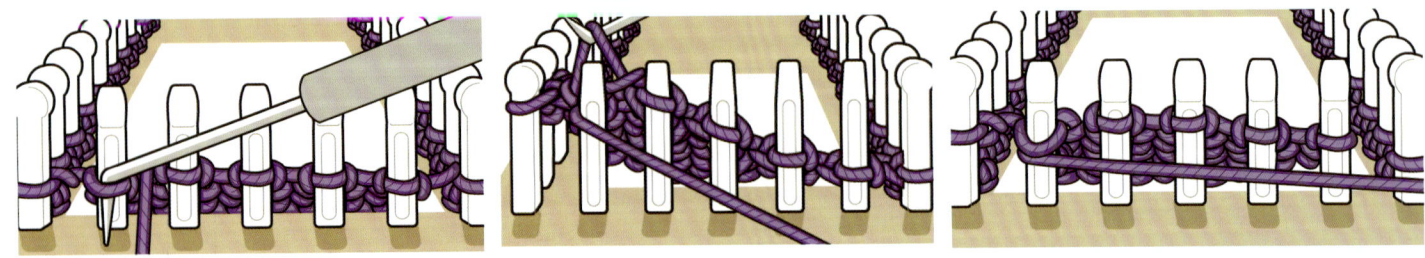

Finishing the Toe

There are 2 ways to remove the sock from the loom and close the toe. One is with a bind off and sewing, which allows the seam to show.

The 2nd is the Kitchener st which will create an invisible closure.

Sewing Closure

Bind off stitches or remove stitches from loom.

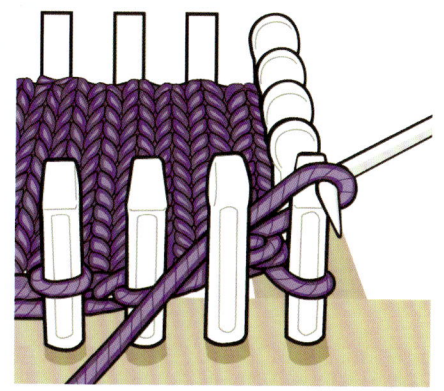 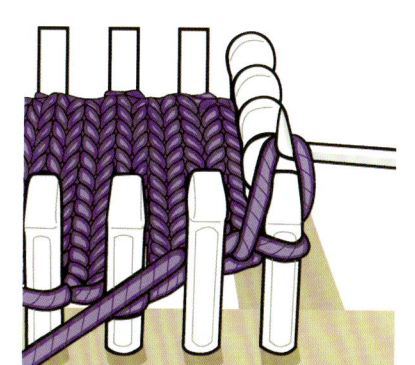 

1. Work the first two pegs. Then take the second stitch off the peg and place it onto the first peg. (2 loops on 1st, 2nd is empty)

2. KO bottom loop, only one loop remains on the first peg.

3. Take this new loop and move it to the empty second peg. The first peg is now bound off.

Repeat steps above, 1-3, except work first peg instead of first 2 pegs. Continue around the loom until last peg. Cut the yarn, leaving a 6 inch yarn tail. Slip the yarn tail through the last peg on the loom, remove this last peg off the loom, and simply pull gently on the yarn tail to secure the last peg.

Closing the toe of your sock: If you bind off the toe edge, you will want to simply sew the edge bind off sts together with matching yarn and tapestry needle.

Using a tapestry needle, begin sewing the opening closed with the whip stitch or invisible stitch. Line up the toe so that the sock is in correct position; starting from end with yarn attached, pick up the inside of the stitches with sewing needle. Work your bind off stitches with even spacing, so that the seam lays nice and flat.

Kitchener Stitch (Grafting)

This will create a seamless closure. (Do not use bind off). You will move stitches from your loom onto 2 double pointed knitting needles. Place the instep stitches, (half of your pegs) onto one double pointed knitting needle. Place the remaining stitches, sole stitches, onto second double pointed needle.

Set up: Needle closest to you will be known as the "Front needle". Needle behind will be known as "Back needle". Use tapestry needle with matching sock yarn to sew the loops off the needles. Start the sewing at right side of double pointed needles.

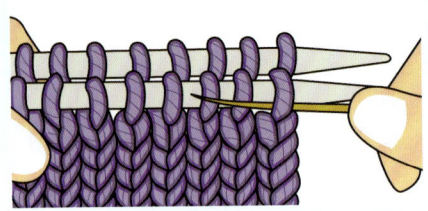

1. Insert tapestry needle through the first stitch from the RIGHT side of st, on the FRONT NEEDLE as if to purl. Leave stitch on the knitting needle.

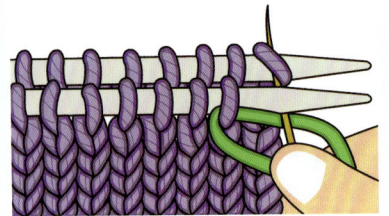

2. Insert tapestry needle through the first stitch from the LEFT side of st on BACK NEEDLE as if to knit. Leave stitch on the knitting needle. Now set up is complete.

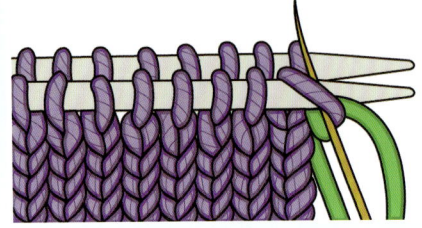

3. FRONT NEEDLE: Insert tapestry needle through first stitch from the LEFT side of st (as if to knit); take stitch off the knitting needle.

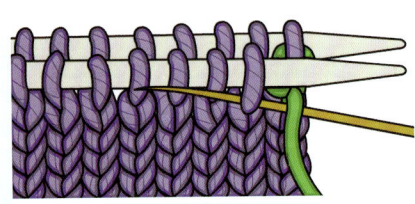

4. FRONT NEEDLE: Insert tapestry needle through first stitch from the RIGHT side of st (as if to purl); leave stitch on the needle.

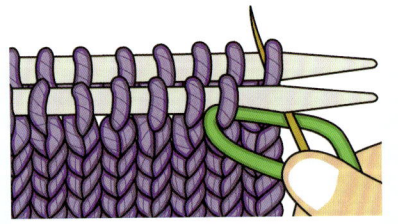

5. BACK NEEDLE: Insert tapestry needle through first stitch from the RIGHT side of st (as if to purl); take stitch off the knitting needle.

6. BACK NEEDLE: Insert tapestry needle through first stitch from the LEFT side of st (as if to knit); leave stitch on the needle.

Repeat steps 3-6 until all sts have been removed. Weave in the end tails.

Seaming Techniques

In single knitting, it is important to block knit pieces before seaming them together. Lay knit down edge to edge, right side up, on a flat surface and then follow steps below.

Joining 2 Edge Stockinette Rows
(Mattress Stitch)

Insert the needle between the loops of the edge st and pick up the horizontal bar or the yarn going across the stitch. With this bar on the needle, pick up the same bar on edge st on opposite knit piece. Pull these sts together and continue along the edges joining in same manner.

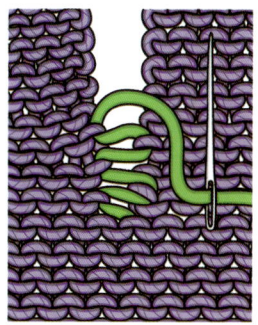

Joining 2 Edge Garter Rows

These edges have both knit and purl edge stitches. Insert the needle into the top loop on one knit edge, then in the bottom loop of the st on the other piece. Continue alternating in this manner.

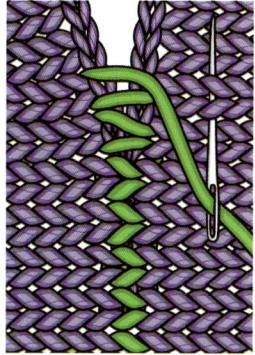

Joining Bound-Off Edges Together
(Horizontal to Horizontal Knit)

Insert the yarn needle under a stitch inside the bound-off edge of one side and then under the same stitch on the other side. Then pull yarn tight to hide the bound off edges.

Joining Bind-Off Edges to a Row
(Horizontal to Vertical Knit)

This is joining one bound off edge, to a soft knit row. Insert the needle under the stitch beside the bound-off edge, and then under 1 or 2 horizontal strands between the 1st and 2nd row on the knit row (vertical). Pull together, and then continue alternating to create seam.

Getting Started...

Simple Ribbed Sock Pattern

This pattern will illustrate all the sections of knitting a sock. A great pattern for your first loom knit sock.

Knitting Loom: Fine gauge sock loom with 52 pegs (KB Sock Loom, fine gauge, used in sample)

Size: Fits 8.5" foot circumference. If foot is a different size use chart on page 6 for correct peg number.

Yarn: Approx 350 yards of fingering weight yarn. Knit Picks stroll tonal used in sample (1 skein springtime).

Notions: Knitting tool, tapestry needle, 2 double pointed needles, size 2 (to aid in grafting).

Gauge: 7 sts x 10 rows=1" in stockinette.

Cast on 52 pegs.

Cuff: Knit (1) stitch and purl (3) stitches and then repeat all around the loom until cuff is 1", or desired height. (Tip: Use stitch markers, or lay down masking tape on loom to mark which pegs to knit.)

Another cuff option is a rolled cuff you create by simply continuing in k st or f st after you cast on.

Leg: After cuff of sock is complete you are ready to work the leg. Continue in k st or f st until leg section is 6" in length. If a longer sock is desired, knit additional rnds.

Heel, Part 1

The heel uses half (1/2) of the pegs that are used for the sock, one long side and the stationary short side of the loom.

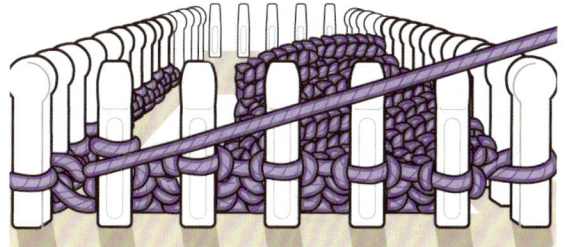

1. Start with the beginning peg on the long side. Work each peg to the last peg on the short side, peg #26. Do not work this last peg. Wrap and Turn this peg.

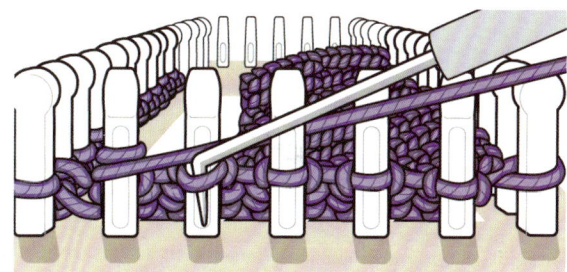

2. Work each peg, working back in the opposite direction.

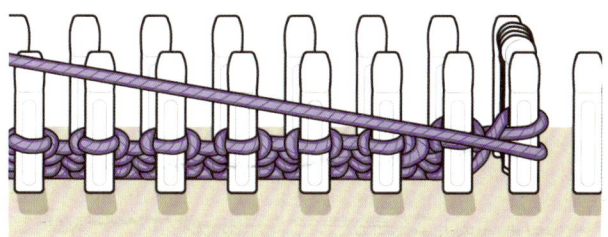

3. Work back to the beginning peg. Do not work this first peg. Wrap and Turn 1st peg.

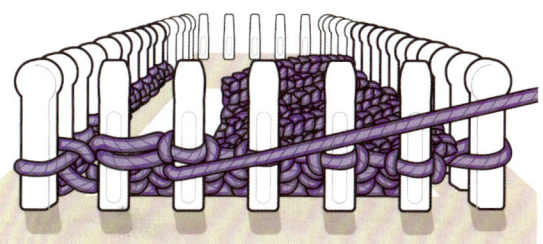

4. Then continue working back to peg before the last wrapped peg. Wrap and Turn on this peg.

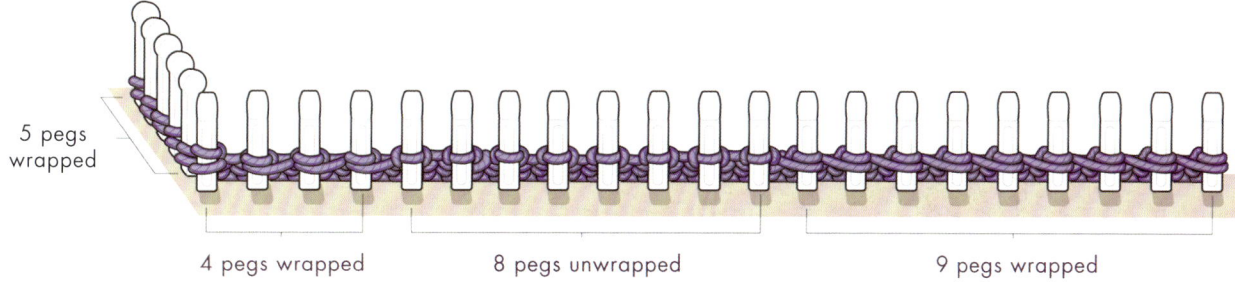

5 pegs wrapped

4 pegs wrapped   8 pegs unwrapped   9 pegs wrapped

5. Continue wrapping and working back and forth until you have wrapped 2/3 of the heel pegs. When using 26 sts for the heel, this means that the first 9 stitches are wrapped and the middle 8 are unwrapped, and the last 9 pegs are wrapped.

Heel, Part 2

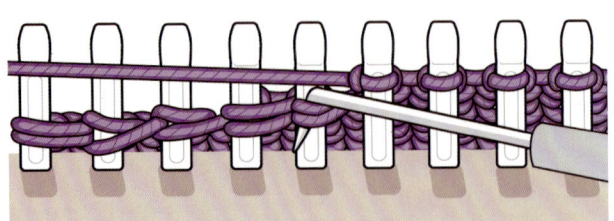

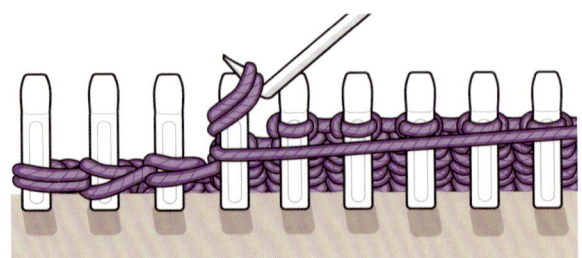

6. The second part of the heel process is to work back on these wrapped stitches. Continue to work the middle, unwrapped stitches until you come to the first wrapped stitch.

7. Then wrap the next peg again. Lift the stitch and the wrap, wrap the peg, and then put both loops back on peg. There will now be 3 loops on this peg. Turn and knit until you reach the first wrapped peg. Knit this peg and then wrap next peg, being careful to get all loops back on the peg.

8. Now continue in this process, working all stitches back and forth until you reach the last wrapped stitch. Work this peg and then wrap the peg outside of the heel pegs.

Once the heel is complete, it is a good idea to add extra reinforcement to each side of sock at beginning and end of heel. To do this, work with stitch on peg adjacent to first and last peg of heel. These 2 pegs are not part of the heel pegs. Pick up the previous stitch (located at base, inside of these pegs). Place it on the first and last heel pegs so that these 2 pegs have 2 loops. When starting the foot of the sock, be sure to work the 2 loops over one on the 1st and last heel pegs and the pegs just outside of the heel pegs.

Note: When creating the short rows in the heel and toe, lift the wraps over before you lift the stitch over on the wrapped pins. This will give the sock a nicer look.

Foot of Sock: Continue in the working stitch for the length of your foot. (In general, measure the length of your foot in inches and then subtract 2". This will be how many inches to knit your foot before starting the toe.)

Toe: The toe is worked using the same method as the heel. Work the long rows and short rows on half of your stitches. Complete all steps. Be sure to start the toe on same starting peg as you used to start the heel so that the heel and toe are lined up.

Now you are ready to finish the toe. Use either the kitchener stitch or bind off and sew the toe. Then weave in ends. Your sock is complete.

Resizing a Sock Pattern

Most sock patterns are written for a specific size sock, but you can make the adjustments for the size desired and still use the pattern that you have chosen. Remember, the size around the opening of the sock is determined by how many pegs you initially cast on. Be sure to increase or decrease this amount of pegs used by a multiple of the stitch pattern used in the design.

Example: If the stitch pattern calls for knit 2, purl 2 for a rib stitch pattern, you will need to increase or decrease by multiples of 4 in order to have a uniform ribbing.

Once you have completed the cuff of the sock, you are ready to knit the leg. You can do as many rows or inches as desired for the height of the sock. For instance, if the pattern says to work in knit stitch for 3 inches or 15 rounds and you want the sock closer to the knee, you can continue working until the sock is as tall as desired. Similarly, after working the heel, you can shorten or lengthen the foot of the sock by adjusting the amount of rounds or inches that you knit before working the toe. Just remember that the toe adds about 2" to the length of the sock, so measure accordingly when determining how long to knit the foot.

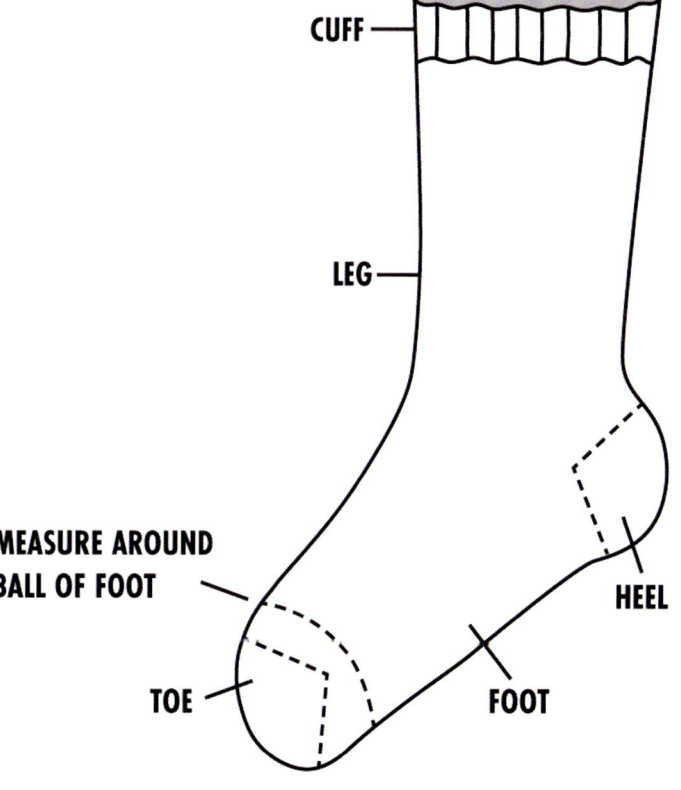

CUFF

LEG

MEASURE AROUND
BALL OF FOOT

HEEL

TOE

FOOT

Men's Tube Socks

Love to knit socks but want a super fast pattern that doesn't use the heel process? Tube socks are a staple in anyone's sock drawer. Fun to knit and fun to wear!

Materials

Knitting Loom: Regular gauge sock loom with 52 pegs (KB Sock Loom② used in sample).

Size: Fits 9.5" foot circumference.

Yarn: Approx 350 yards of worsted weight yarn. Sample used Knit Picks Wool of the Andes Worsted in Deft Heather (3 skeins) and White (1 skein). MC=Deft Heather CC=White

Notions: Knitting tool, tapestry needle, 2 double pointed needles size 5 (to aid in grafting).

Gauge: 5.5 sts x 7 rows= 1" in stockinette.

Instructions

Cuff

Using MC, CO 52 sts, join to work in the rnd.

Work in Ribbing Stitch for 1".

Leg

Continue in St st for another ½".

Join CC, work 3 rnds in St st. Do not cut yarn.

PU MC, work 2 rnds in St st. Do not cut yarn.

PU CC, work 3 rnd in St st. Cut CC, leaving a 6" yarn tail.

PU MC, continue in St st until piece measures 20" from CO edge.

Toe

Next rnd: *k2tog; rep from * to end. (26 sts remain) Move loop from peg 1 to peg 2, 3 to peg 4, 5 to peg 6, and so on, until every odd numbered peg is empty. Move all the loops inward so that there are no empty pegs. When working the pegs, make sure to treat both loops on the peg as one loop. Reset your knitting loom to the new peg number by sliding your end pieces inwards

Next rnd: K to the end.

Next rnd: *k2tog; rep from * to end. (13 sts remain)

GBO (Gather Bind Off).

You'll enjoy knitting up many pairs of these easy socks in lots of colors for the entire family.

Ribbing Stitch

Rnd 1: *k2, p2; rep from * to end.
Rep Rnd 1.

Stockinette (St st)

Rnd 1: *k; rep from * to end.
Rep Rnd.

Gather Bind Off (GBO):

Take a threaded tapestry needle and pick up first stitch from peg 1 and continue picking up all stitches, removing them from the loom. Cinch together and knot. Weave in ends.

TIP

When creating stripes, it is nice for the stripes not to look like a small step at the beginning of the round. To avoid this "step" look, knit the stitch from the round below with the stitch from the current round, this eliminates that "step" you get when creating stripes.

Ruffles for Me Socks

Put a little bounce in her step with these adorable ruffle socks. A fun and easy pattern for beginner sock knitters, and a design loved by all ages!

Materials

Knitting Loom: Fine gauge sock loom with 40 pegs (KB Sock Loom used in sample).

Size: Fits 6" foot circumference (approx. 5-6 year old).

Yarn: Approx. 160 yards of fingering weight yarn. Sample used Knit Picks Palette in Green and Pink. 1 skein of each color. CC=Pink MC=Green

Notions: Knitting tool, tapestry needle, 2 double pointed needles size 5 (to aid in grafting).

Gauge: 8 sts x 12 rows= 1" in stockinette.

Instructions

Stockinette Stitch

Rnd 1: *k rep from * to end

Rep Rnd 1

Garter Stitch

Rnd 1: *k, rep from * to end.

Rnd 2: *p, rep from * to end.

Rep Rnds 1 and 2."

Cuff

Using CC, CO 20 sts, prepare to knit a flat panel.

Work in garter stitch until piece measures 12".

BO, leaving a 20" yarn tail for seaming later. Set aside.

Leg

Using MC, CO 40 sts, join to work in the round.

Work in St st until leg measures 2" from CO edge, or desired length.

Heel

- Work heel back and forth in short rows on 20 sts. Reference Heel on page 15.

- After first part of heel is complete, 7 stitches will be wrapped, 6 unwrapped and 7 wrapped. Then follow second part of heel process.

- After the heel, the pegs adjacent to the 1st and last heel pegs (peg 40 and 21) will have 1 wrap each. Begin working in rnd for foot, but on those pegs, knit the two loops over the one.

Foot

Continue working in St st for foot, until sole measures 5" from back of heel, or 1.5" from desired length.

Toe

Work toe back and forth in short rows on 20 sts. Follow same instructions as for Heel.

Knit one last row, picking up the wraps on the first and last pegs.

Finishing

Sew the end of the toes together by using the grafting technique.

Arrange needles as follows: Place the top 20 sts (instep stitches) on one needle. Place the remaining 20 sts (sole) on another needle. Needles are prepped for grafting.

Graft the toes.

Using tapestry needle, sew the ruffle to the CO edge of the leg.

TIP

Seam two garter stitch ridges to every stitch on the leg. Weave ends in.

Sideways Socks

A simple twist in the cuff adds detail and texture to these beautiful socks. You won't need to worry about a sock that slides down your leg because the cuff wraps around the ankles. Fits like a dream-you'll want to have several of these for yourself as well as gifts for the family.

Materials

Knitting Loom: Regular gauge sock loom with 40 pegs, (KB Sock Loom② used in sample).

Size: Fits 8 1/2" foot circumference.

Yarn: 280 yards of worsted weight yarn. Sample used Knit Picks Swish Worsted in Peapod, 3 skeins.

Notions: Knitting tool, tapestry needle, 2 double pointed needles size 5 (to aid in grafting).

Gauge: 6 sts x 6 rows=1" in stockinette.

Size: Fits 8 ½" foot circumference.

Instructions

Cuff (worked lengthways)

This is worked in a flat panel.

CO 22 sts.

Row 1: Work from Cable Chart on first 8 sts. K to the end.

Row 2: Knit to last 8 sts. Work from Cable Chart on last 8 sts.

Row 3: Work from Cable Chart on first 8 sts. K to the end.

Row 4: Knit to last 8 sts. Work from Cable Chart on last 8 sts.

Rep Rows 1-4 until piece measures 9.5". BO. (This should fit snuggly around ankle, so adjust as needed. It will need to fit to the top of sock without stretching or binding when you sew the 2 pieces together.

Mattress stitch seam CO edge to BO edge. Set aside.

Leg

CO 40 sts, join to work in the rnd.

Continue in St st for another 1 ½".

Heel

- Work heel back and forth in short rows on the first 20 sts. Reference Heel on page 15.

- After first part of heel is complete, 7 stitches will be wrapped, 6 unwrapped and 7 wrapped. Then follow second part of heel process.

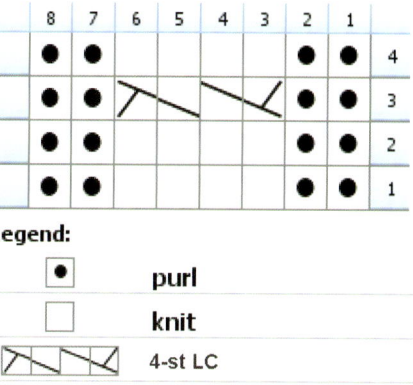

Legend:

•	purl
	knit
⟋⟍	4-st LC

4-st LC Cable

Step 1: Take working yarn behind pegs 1 and 2 (you are skipping pegs 1 and 2).

Step 2: Knit pegs 3 and 4, transfer these stitches to cable needle.

Step 3: Take working yarn to the front of peg 1, knit pegs 1 and 2.

Step 4: Transfer the stitches as follows: move stitch from peg 2 to peg 4, move stitch from peg 1 to peg 3.

Step 5: Transfer the stitches from the cable needle and place them on pegs 1 and 2. With your knitting tool, gently pull on stitches to take up any slack in yarn tension and tighten the stitches.

- After the heel, the pegs adjacent to the 1st and last heel pegs (peg 40 and 21) will have 1 wrap each. Begin working in rnd for foot, but on those pegs, knit the two loops over the one.

Foot

Continue working in St st for foot, until sole measures 7" from back of heel, or longer if desired.

Toe

Work toe back and forth in short rows on the first 20 sts. Follow same instructions as for Heel. Make sure to use the same pegs as used for heel.

Finishing

Using the mattress stitch, seam the cuff to the body of the sock with the cable design edge at the top of the sock. Ease this seam together so that you will not stretch the seam when pulling on the sock.

Yoga Socks

The perfect companion to your yoga mat, a warm and cozy pair of socks that will keep your feet toasty.

Materials

Knitting Loom: Fine gauge sock loom with 50 pegs (KB Sock Loom used in sample).

Size: Fits 8" foot circumference.

Yarn: Approx. 350 yards of fingering weight yarn. Sample used Knit Picks Stroll Tranquil in fingering weight.

Notions: Knitting tool, tapestry needle.

Gauge: 8 sts x 12 rows= 1" in stockinette.

Single Ribbing Stitch

Rnd 1: *k1, p1; rep from * to end.
Rep Rnd 1.

Instructions

Cuff

CO 50 sts, join to work in the rnd.

Work in Single Ribbing Stitch for 1".

Leg

Work in Wigwam Lace Stitch Pattern until leg measures 6" from CO edge.

Next rnd: BO 25 sts, continue Wigwam Lace Stitch Pattern on remaining 25 sts.

Next rnd: CO 25 sts, continue Wigwam Lace Stitch Pattern on the next 25 sts.

Foot

Continue working in Wigwam Lace Stitch Pattern for foot (50 sts), until sole measures 6.5 inches from BO edge.

Next 3 rnds: Single Ribbing Stitch

BO with Basic Bind Off method.

Weave ends in. Block lightly.

10	9	8	7	6	5	4	3	2	1	
										10
		O	λ	O						9
										8
		O	/		\	O				7
										6
O	/					\	O			5
										4
						O	λ	O		3
										2
						O	λ	O		1

Legend:

O	yo
λ	sl1 k2tog psso
(blank)	knit
\	ssk
/	k2tog

Wigwam Lace Stitch Pattern Breakdown

Rnd1: Move stitch from peg 2 to peg 3. Move stitch from peg 1 to peg 2. Ewrap peg 1. Knit peg 3 (treat both loops on peg as 1 loop). Place loop from peg 3 on peg 2. Knit over (lift bottom loop off peg). Ewrap peg 3. Knit from peg 3-10.

Rnd 2 (and every even row): k

Rnd 3: As Rnd 1

Rnd 5: Knit pegs 1-3. Move stitch from peg 5 to peg 4. Knit peg 4. Move stitch from peg 4 to peg 5. Ewrap peg 4. Knit peg 6, 7, 8. Move stitch from peg 9 to peg 10. Knit peg 10. Move stitch from peg 10 to peg 9. Ewrap peg 10.

Rnd 7: Knit pegs 1-4. Move stitch from peg 6 to peg 5. Knit peg 5. Move stitch from peg 5 to peg 6. Ewrap peg 5. Knit peg 7. Move stitch from peg 8 to peg 9. Knit peg 9. Move stitch from peg 9 to peg 8. Ewrap peg 9. Knit peg 10.

Rnd 9: Knit pegs 1-5. Move stitch from peg 7 to peg 8. Move stitch from peg 6 to peg 7. Ewrap peg 6.

Knit peg 8 (treat both loops on peg as 1 loop). Place loop from peg 8 on peg 7. Knit over (lift bottom loop off peg). Ewrap peg 8. Knit pegs 9 and 10.

Peaks Fingerless Mitts

A gorgeous winter accessory to bring some warmth to your hands while keeping your fingers accessible for daily tasks. These mitts combine warm, soft colors with a beautiful design.

Materials

Knitting Loom: Fine gauge sock loom with 48 pegs (KB Sock Loom used in sample).

Size: 6" circumference, 7.75" length.

Yarn: Approx 150 yards of sock weight yarn. Sample used Patons Kroy Socks Stripes in Sweet Stripes, (1 skein).

Notions: Knitting tool, tapestry needle.

Gauge: 7.5 sts x 9 rows= 1" in stockinette.

Instructions

CO 48, join to work in the rnd.

Prep round: p

Rnd 1-20: Follow Peaks Stitch Pattern

Next 28 rnds: k

Next rnd: Remove the first 8 sts from pegs and place on stitch holder (pegs 1-8). Using the e-wrap method, CO 8 sts on emptied pegs, k to end.

Next 7 rnds: k

Next 10 rnds: Work Peaks Stitch Pattern.

Next rnd: p

Next rnd: k

BO

Thumb Instructions

Set up knitting loom to 20 sts in the round.

Place the 8 sts from the stitch holder back on the knitting loom on pegs 1-8.

TIP

Insert the thumb opening through the center of the loom, from the bottom up.

Next: k8, pick up 12sts and join to work in the rnd.

Next 10 rnds: k

Next rnd: k

Next rnd: p

BO for thumb opening.

Weave ends in. Block lightly.

Peaks Stitch Pattern

Row 1: k.

Row 2: k1, yo, k2, sl1-k2tog-psso, k2, yo.

Breakdown (over 8 stitches) of the above stitch pattern.

Row 1: k8

Row 2: Knit peg 1. Ewrap peg 1 (this loop will eventually be moved to peg 2).

Knit peg 2 and peg 3.

Skip peg 4.

Move loop from peg 5 to peg 6. Knit peg 6. Move loop from peg 4 to peg 5. Move loop from peg 6 over to peg 5. Lift the bottom-most loop on peg 5.

Move loop from peg 3 to peg 4.

Move loop from peg 2 to peg 3.

Move the ewrap on peg 1 to peg 2.

Move loops from peg 7 to peg 6, loop from peg 8 to peg 7.

Knit pegs 6 and 7.

Ewrap peg 8.

Monkey Socks

The classic monkey socks will keep your little one's toes warm and toasty. These can be worn as slippers on a cold morning watching Saturday cartoons.

Materials

Knitting Loom: Regular Gauge Sock Loom with 36 pegs (KB Sock Loom② used in sample).

Size: Fits up to 6 ½" foot circumference.

Yarn: Approx 225 yards of worsted weight yarn. Sample used Patons Classic Wool in colors Aran (1/4 of a skein), Natural Mix (1 skein) and Bright Red (1/8 of a skein).

Notions: Knitting tool, tapestry needle, 2 double pointed needles size 5 (to aid in grafting).

Gauge: 6 sts x 7 rows= 1" in stockinette.

Instructions

Cuff

Using CC, CO 36 sts, join to work in the round.

Work in Single Ribbing Stitch Pattern for ¾".

Leg

Join MC, cut CC leaving a 6" yarn tail. Continue in St st until Leg measures 5" from CO edge.

Heel

- Follow short row heel instructions page 15.

- Join SCC, do not cut MC. Work heel with SCC back and forth in short rows using 18 pegs.

- After first part of heel is complete, 6 stitches will be wrapped, 6 unwrapped and 6 wrapped. Then follow second part of heel process.

- After the heel, the pegs adjacent to the first and last heel peg (pegs 36 and 19) will have extra wraps on them. When working the sole, on that first round work those extra loops with the stitch as if they were one stitch. Continue to Foot.

- Cut SCC leaving a 6" yarn tail, continue with MC.

Foot

Continue working in St st for foot, until sole measures 5¼" from back of heel (longer if desired).

Toe

Cut MC leaving a 6" yarn tail, join CC. Work toe in CC back and forth in short rows on 18 sts.

Follow same instructions as for Heel. Be sure to start on same beginning peg.

Finishing

Sew the end of the toes together by using the kitchener stitch.

Weave ends in. Block lightly.

Single Ribbing Stitch

Rnd 1: *k1, p1; rep from * to end.
Rep Rnd 1.

Stockinette Stitch (St st)

Rnd 1: *k; rep from * to end.
Rep Rnd 1.

Join 2 Colors: Cut yarn leaving a 6" tail, attach new yarn, (leaving a 6" tail) by making a temporary knot. Begin knitting with new yarn. After item is complete, remove temporary knot and weave ends in.

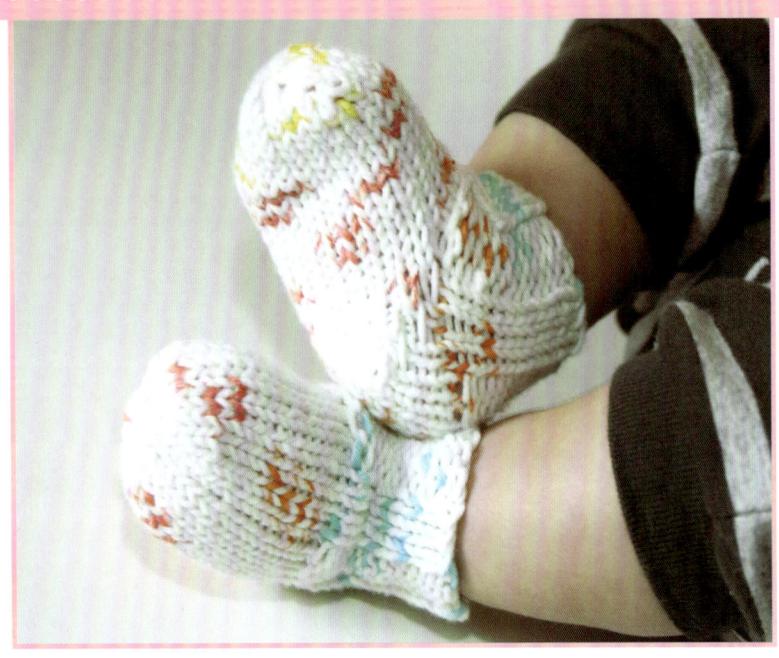

Baby's First Socks

Simply soft and lovely itty bitty socks for baby. Knit in ribbing for a comfortable fit around the legs and simple stockinette for the sole and toes.

Materials

Knitting Loom: Regular gauge sock loom with 30 pegs (KB Sock Loom② used in sample).

Size: 0-3 (3-6) months. Sample shows 0-3 months.

Yarn: Approx. 40 yards of Light/DK weight yarn. Lion Brand Casey in Rainbow Spots was used in sample.

Notions: Tapestry needle, knitting tool.

Gauge: 6 sts x 8 rows = 1"

Instructions

Cuff

CO 24 (30) sts.

Rnd 1: *k3, p3; rep from * to end

Rep Rnd 1 until leg measures 1.5" (1.75").

Next rnd: k to the end. Continue to heel.

Heel

● Work heel in short rows on the first 12 (15) sts. Refer to Heel on page 15.

● After first part of heel is complete, 4 stitches will be wrapped, 4 unwrapped and 4 wrapped or (5,5, and 5). Then follow second part of heel process.

● After the heel, the pegs adjacent to the first and last heel peg (pegs 24 and 13; pegs 30, and 16) will have extra wraps on them. When working the sole, on that first round work those extra loops with the stitch as if they were one stitch. Continue to Foot.

Foot

Begin working the round once again.

Next rnd: k (be sure to pick up the wraps from pegs 24, 13; 30, 16 on this first round of the sole).

Next rnd: k

Rep last rnd until sole measures 3" (3.5").

Toe

**Next rnd: k to end of the rnd, decrease 4 stitches around evenly.

Move stitch from peg 1 to peg 24. Move stitch from peg 7 to peg 8 (corner slider peg). Move stitch from peg 13 to peg 12 (corner slider peg), from peg 19 to 20. The 4 corner pegs now have 2 loops on them. Slide the slider inwards 2 pegs spacing, move the loops to occupy the empty pegs, 2 to 1, 3 to 2, etc.

Next rnd: k **

Repeat from ** to ** 2 more times, (12, (18)) stitches remain.

Gather Bind Off (GBO), refer to page 20 for GBO.

Weave in ends.

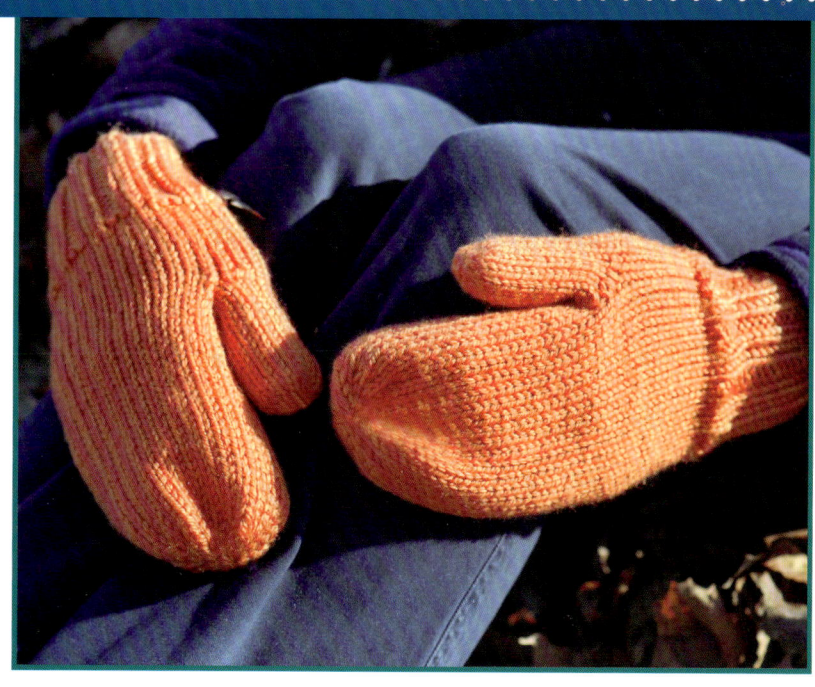

His & Hers Mittens

Basic Mitten Pattern for men and women. Stay toasty warm this winter with your comfy mittens.

Materials

Knitting Loom: Regular gauge sock loom with 48 pegs for mens and 36 pegs for women, (KB Sock Loom② used in sample).

Size: Fits average adult Women (Men).

Yarn: Approx 250 yards of worsted weight yarn for each size. Sample uses Red Heart Soft in Tangerine (Leaf).

Notions: Knitting tool, tapestry needle, stitch holder.

Gauge: 5.5 sts x 12.5 rows= 1" in stockinette.

Instructions

CO 36 (48) sts, join to work in the rnd, continue with Ribbed Cuff instructions.

Ribbed Cuff

Rnds 1-20 (24): *k2, p2; rep from * to end.

Cuff completed, continue with Hand instructions. Note: if you desire a longer cuff, work more rounds for the cuff.

Hand

Next 20 (25) rnds: k to end.

Next rnd: Place first 6 (8) sts on a stitch holder. CO 6 (8) sts, k to the end.

Next 28 (32) rnds: k to end.

Next rnd: *k2tog; rep from * to end.

Move loop from peg 1 to peg 2, 3 to peg 4, 5 to peg 6, and so on, until every odd numbered peg is empty. Move all the loops inward so that there are no empty pegs. When working the pegs, make sure to treat both loops on the peg as one loop.

Reset your knitting loom to the new peg number by sliding the slider inwards.

Next rnd: k to end.

Women size ends here.

GBO for women (Refer to GBO on page 20). Men's size continue.

Next rnd: *k2tog; rep from * to end

Next rnd: k

GBO for men.

TIP
Insert the thumb opening through the center of the loom opening from the bottom up.

Thumb Instructions

Set up knitting loom to 16 (20) sts in the round.

Place the 6 (8) sts from the stitch holder back on the knitting loom.

Next: k6 (8), pick up 10 (12) sts and place back on the loom.

Next 15 (18) rnds: k to end.

GBO.

Weave ends in. Block lightly.

Pattern Note

Pattern is provided for women (men). When only one set of instructions is provided, follow for both; instructions inside parenthesis are for men size only.

Men sample shown in Leaf colorway. Women sample shown in Tangerine colorway.

Farrow Rib Socks

A simple modified rib pattern provides texture to this cozy pair of socks.

Thin ribs down the leg make a really well-fitting sock that stays in place.

Materials

Knitting Loom: Fine gauge sock loom with 60 pegs (KB Sock Loom used in sample).

Size: Fits 9" to 9.5" foot circumference.

Yarn: Approx 380 yards of fingering weight yarn. Sample used Malabrigo sock weight in Lettuce, 1 skein.

Notions: Knitting tool, tapestry needle, 2 double pointed needles size 2 (to aid in grafting).

Gauge: 8 sts x 12 rows=1" in stockinette.

Instructions

Cuff

Cast on 60 sts, join to work in the round.

Round 1-15: *k2, p1; rep from * to end of rnd.

Leg

Follow Farrow Rib Stitch Pattern, until leg measures 8" from beginning of Farrow Rib stitch pattern. End on Rnd 2. Total leg length with cuff is 9.25".

Heel

- Work heel back and forth in short rows on 30 sts (first 30 stitches). Reference page 15.

- After first part of heel is complete, 10 stitches will be wrapped, 10 unwrapped and 10 wrapped. Then follow second part of heel process.

- After the heel, the pegs adjacent to the 1st and last heel pegs (peg 60 and 31) will have 1 wrap each. Begin working in rnd for foot, but on those pegs, knit the two loops over the one.

Foot

Work k st on sole of the sock (stitches 1-30). Continue working Farrow Rib pattern on instep (31-60). Work until sole measures 8" from back of heel.

Toe

Work toe back and forth in short rows on 30 sts. Follow same instructions as for Heel. Be sure to start toe on same peg as used in Heel.

Knit one row on the 30 sts, picking up the wraps on the first and last stitch.

Finishing

Sew the end of the toes together by using the kitchener stitch.

Weave ends in. Block lightly.

These socks can be worn with shoes and feel comfortable under slacks and jeans.

Farrow Rib

Rnd 1: *k2, p1; rep from * to end.
Rnd 2: *k1, p2; rep from * to end.
Rep these 2 rows.

Simple Ribbed Socks

These socks are so easy to knit and one of my favorites. Knitted in wool yarn makes them warm and super cozy. Create for the whole family. They will love them.

Materials

Knitting Loom: Regular gauge sock loom with 36 pegs (KB Sock Loom② used in sample).

Size: Fits a foot circumference of up to 9".

Yarn: Approx 180 yards of worsted weight yarn. Knit Picks Chroma Worsted in Galapagos color was used in sample (1 skein).

Notions: Knitting tool, tapestry needle, or 2 double pointed needles size 2 (to aid in grafting).

Gauge: 4.75 sts x 6 rows= 1" in stockinette.

Instructions

CO 36 sts, join to work in the rnd.

Leg

Rnd 1: *p1, k3: rep from * to the end of rnd.

Rep Rnd 1 until leg measures 7" from cast on edge, or desired length.

Heel

- Work back and forth in short rows over 18 pegs pegs, 1-18. Refer to Heel on page 15. After first part of heel is complete, 6 stitches will be wrapped, 6 unwrapped and 6 wrapped. Then follow second part of heel process.

- After the heel, the pegs adjacent to the 1st and last heel pegs (peg 36 and 19) will have 1 wrap each. Begin working in rnd for foot, but on those pegs, knit the two loops over the one.

Foot

Continue knitting in the round as follows:

Next: k20, *p1, k3; rep from * to end.

Repeat last round until sole measures 2" less than desired length.

Next: k

Toe

Work toe back and forth in short rows over 18 sts. Follow same instructions as for Heel.

Then knit one row on the 18 sts, picking up the wraps on the first and last stitch. Cut the yarn leaving an 18" tail.

Finishing

Sew the end of the toes together by using the kitchener stitch.

Weave ends in. Block lightly.

Feather Lace Socks

A lovely lace stitch pattern decorates the leg portion of these beautiful socks. Lots of colors make them fun to wear alone or with short boots. Add a splash of color!

Materials

Knitting Loom: Fine gauge sock loom with 54 pegs (KB Sock Loom used in sample).

Size: Fits 8" foot circumference.

Yarn: Approx 350 yards of fingering weight yarn. Sample used Knit Picks Chroma in Lollipop (1 skein).

Notions: Knitting tool, tapestry needle, 2 double pointed needles size 2 (to aid in grafting).

Gauge: 7 sts x 11 rows= 1" in stockinette.

Ripple Pattern

Rnd 1: *[k2tog] 3 times, [k1, yo] 6 times, [k2tog] 3 times; rep from * to end.

Rnd 2: p

Rnd 3: k

Rnd 4: k

Rep Rnd 1-4.

Breakdown of Stitch Pattern

Over 18 stitches.

Number the pegs as follows from right to left.

18, 17, 16, 15, 14, 13, 12, 11, 10, 9, 8, 7, 6, 5, 4, 3, 2, 1

Rnd 1: *[k2tog] 3 times, [k1, yo] 6 times, [k2tog] 3 times; rep from * to end.

Step 1: Move stitches from peg 1 to peg 2; from peg 3 to peg 4; from peg 5 to peg 6.

Step 2: Knit peg 2 (treat both loops on peg as one loop). Move the loop from peg 2 to peg 1.

Step 3: Knit peg 4 (treat both loops on peg as one loop). Move the loop from peg 4 to peg 2.

Step 4: Knit peg 6 (treat both loops on peg as one loop). Move the loop from peg 6 to peg 3.

Tug gently on the working yarn to tighten any yarn slack. Pegs 4, 5, 6 are empty.

Step 5: Knit peg 7 and move the loop to empty peg 4. YO on peg 5. (Note: YO means ewap the peg, or lay the working yarn in front of the empty peg)

Step 6: Knit peg 8 and move the loop to empty peg 6. YO on peg 7.

Step 7: Knit peg 8 and move the loop to empty peg 8. YO on peg 9.

Step 8: Move stitches from peg 17 to peg 18; from peg 15 to 16; from peg 13 to 14. Move the two loops that are on peg 16 to peg 17; move the two loops that are on peg 14 to peg 16. Pegs 15, 14, 13 are empty.

Step 9: Move stitch from peg 12 to peg 14.

Step 10: Move stitch from peg 11 to peg 12.

Step 11: Knit peg 10. YO on peg 11.

Step 12: Knit peg 12. YO on peg 13.

Step 13: Knit peg 14. YO on peg 15.

Step 14: Knit pegs 16, 17, 18 (treat both loops on each peg as one loop).

Instructions

Cuff

CO 54 sts, join to work in the rnd.

Leg

Work in Ripple Pattern Stitch until leg measures 6" from "tall" ridge on CO edge.

Heel

- Follow Heel steps on page 15.

- Work heel back and forth in short rows on the first 27 pegs. After first part of heel is complete, 9 stitches will be wrapped, 9 unwrapped and 9 wrapped. Then follow second part of heel process.

- After the heel, the pegs adjacent to the 1st and last heel pegs (peg 54 and 28) will have 1 wrap each. Begin working in rnd for foot, but on those pegs, knit the two loops over the one.

Foot

Continue working in St st for foot, until sole measures 7" from back of heel.

Toe

Work toe back and forth in short rows on the first 27 sts. Follow same instructions as for Heel.

Next: Work one more row, picking up the wraps on each of the last stitches.

Finishing

Sew the end of the toes together by using the kitchener stitch.

Weave ends in. Block lightly.

Now, try another pair in different colors. So much fun to wear!

Veranda Socks
(Child Size)

Traditional Fair Isle wrapped around the ankle of these socks are reminiscent of a portico full of flowers.

Materials

Knitting Loom: Fine gauge sock loom with 54 pegs (KB Sock Loom used in sample).

Size: Fits 7" foot circumference.

Yarn: Approx 350 yards of fingering weight yarn. Sample used Knit Picks Stroll Fingering in Tranquil, Dandelion, and Eggplant, 1 skein of each. MC= Tranquil CC= Eggplant SCC= Dandelion

Notions: Knitting tool, tapestry needle, 2 double pointed needles size 2 (to aid in grafting).

Gauge: 8 sts x 12 rows= 1" in stockinette.

Instructions

Cuff

Using MC (Tranquil), CO 54 sts, join to work in the rnd.

Work in Single Ribbing Stitch for approx 1".

Leg

Rnds 1-6: Work Colorwork Chart

Rep Rnds 1-6: 6 more times.

Next: Work Rnd 1 of Colorwork Chart.

Heel

● Cut SCC leaving a 6"yarn tail. Tie on CC and work heel. See Join 2 Colors, page 34.

● Follow heel instructions on page 15. Work heel back and forth in short rows on pegs 1-27.

● When first part of heel is complete, 9 pegs will be wrapped, 9 pegs unwrapped and 9 pegs wrapped. Then continue with second part of heel process.

● When heel is complete, your adjacent pegs to 1st and last heel pegs will have a wrap (pegs 54 and 28). Be sure when working these pegs, lift 2 loops over 1.

● Cut CC (Eggplant), leave a 6" yarn tail.

Foot

Work foot with MC (Tranquil).

Continue working in k st for foot, until sole measures 5.5" from back of heel or desired length.

Cut MC (Tranquil), leave a 6" yarn tail. Join CC (Eggplant)

Single Ribbing Stitch

Rnd 1: *k1, p1; rep from * to end.

Rep Rnd 1.

Colorwork

Over 6 sts.

Work in rounds, follow chart below. Read chart from bottom to top, from right to left.

Working with Colors

Carry both yarns together. When the chart/pattern calls for the main color, work the pegs with the main color, when it calls for the contrasting color, drop the MC and bring the CC yarn above the MC yarn, work the stitches as instructed in the pattern. When the pattern calls again for the MC, drop the CC, reach below the CC yarn for the MC yarn. Whenever you change yarns, reach below the working yarn for the "new" yarn that needs to be used.

Toe

Work toe back and forth in short rows on 27 sts. Follow same instructions as for Heel.

Next: Work one more row, picking up the wraps on each of the last stitches.

Finishing

Sew the end of the toes together by using the kitchener stitch.

TIP

When doing Fair Isle colorwork, it is imperative to carry the unused yarn loosely behind the pegs. Failure to carry the yarn loosely will produce a very tight tube.

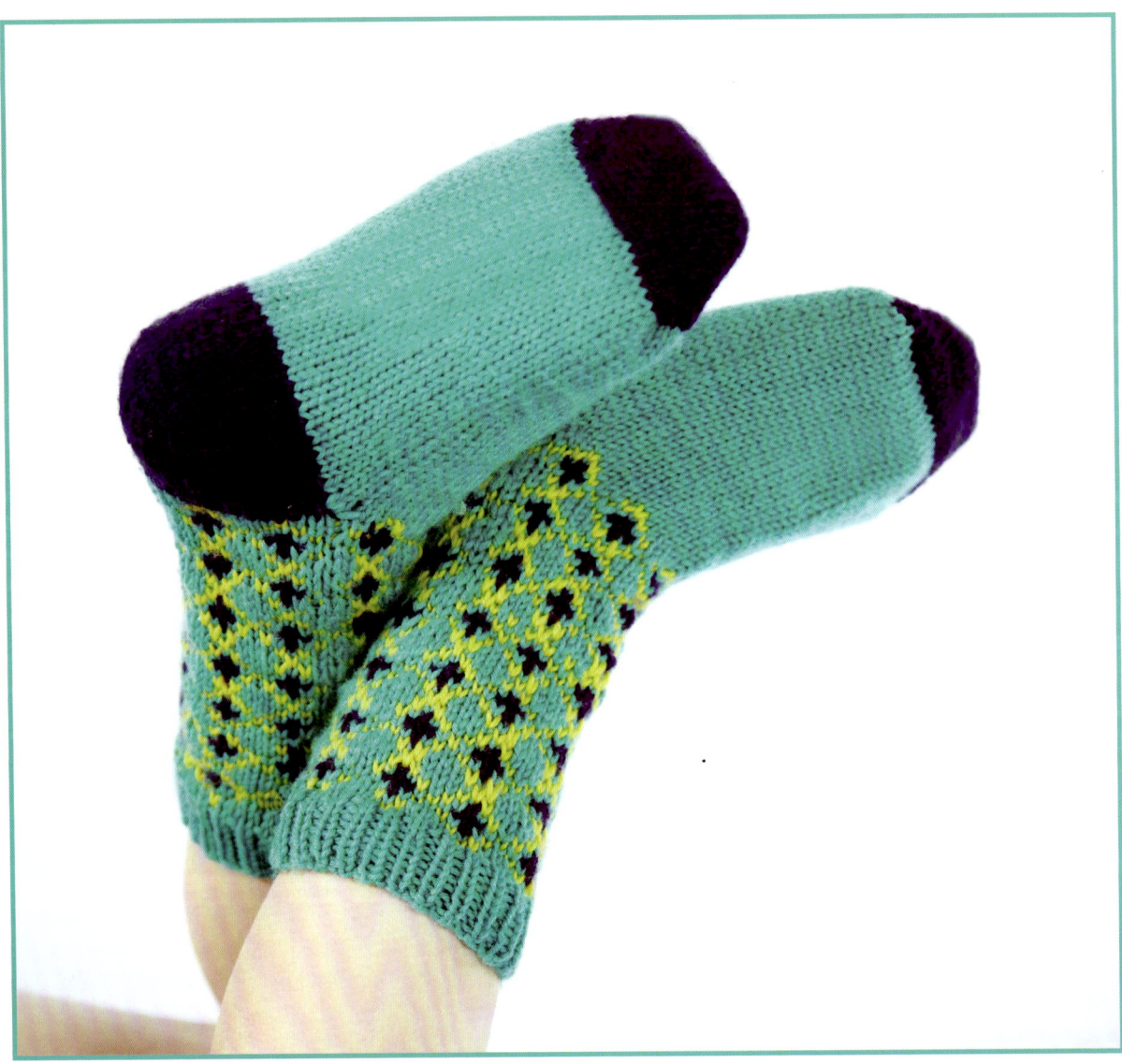

Leg Warmers

Add a splash of color and statement to your wardrobe. These leg warmers are cozy and warm and yet stylish. Pair them up with boots and a skirt, or wear them over tights and you are set.

Materials

Knitting Loom: Regular gauge sock loom with 52 pegs (KB Sock Loom② used in sample).

Size: Fits a calf circumference of up to 12.5", snuggly.

Yarn: 250 yards of worsted weight wool yarn. Knit Picks Chroma in Galapagos (1.5 skeins) was used in sample.

Notions: Knitting tool, tapestry needle.

Gauge: 5 sts x 7 rows= 1" in stockinette.

CO 52 sts, work in the round.

Rnd 1-16: *k4, p4; rep from * to last 4 sts, k4

Rnd 17: k4, p4, *4-st LC, p4, rep from * to last 4 sts, k4 (see Cable 4-st LC instruction on page 25)

Rnd 18-20: *k4, p4; rep from * to last 4 sts, k4

Rep Rnds 17-20: 3 more times.

Rep Rnd 1 until tube measures 15" from CO edge.

BO.

Weave ends in. Block lightly.

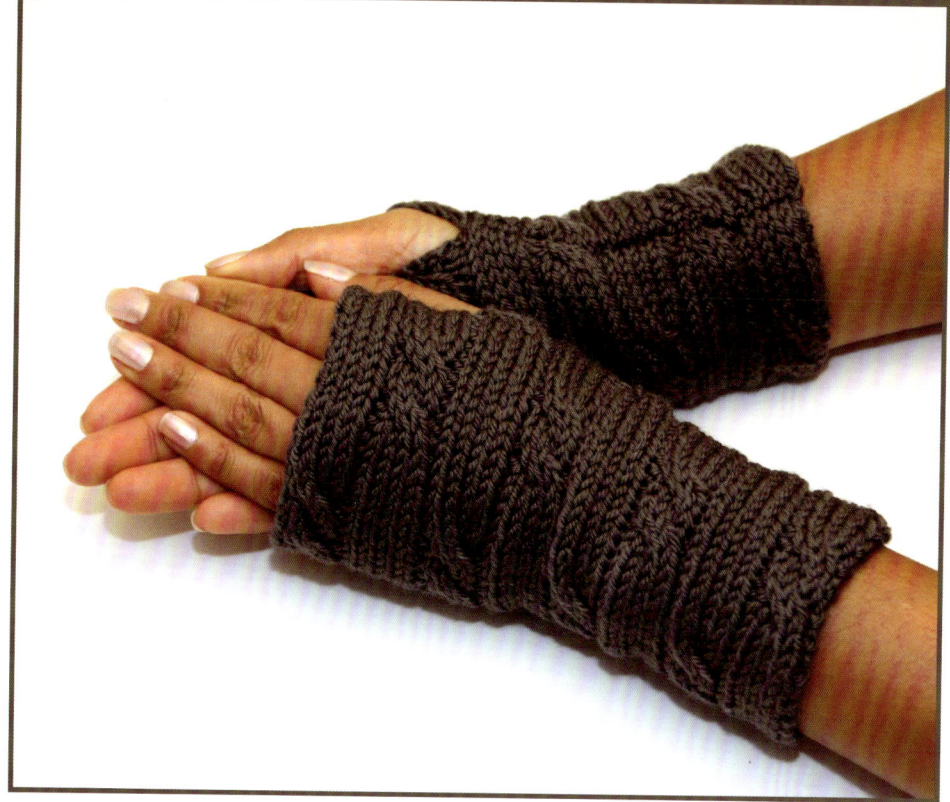

Cable Wristers

Materials

Knitting Loom: Sock loom, regular gauge with 41 pegs (sample uses KB Sock Loom②).

Size: 7" length x 6" circumference

Yarn: 120 yards of chunky weight yarn. Debbie Bliss Cashmerino Chunky in 17033 color was used in sample.

Gauge: 4.5 sts x 7.5 rows = 1" in stockinette stitch

Pattern Note

The fingerless mitts are worked as a flat panel. Once the flat panel is completed, the cast on edge is seamed invisibly to the bind off edge.

The Cable, left cross over 4 stitches (4-st LC) is explained on page 25.

Instructions (Make 2)

CO 41 sts, prepare to knit a flat panel.

Rows 1, 5, 7, 9, 13, 17, 19 and 21: *p1, k4; rep from *, end p1.

Row 2 and all even rows: p1, *k4, p1; rep from * to end.

Rows 3 and 23: *p1, 4-st LC, p1, k4; rep from *, end p1.

Rows 11 and 15: *p1, k4, p1, 4-st LC; rep from *, end p1.

Row 24: Rep row 2.

Rep rows 1-24.

BBO, leaving a 2 yard tail.

Seam

Invisibly stitch seam the cast on edge to the bind off edge as follows: seam 1-inch, then leave approx 1-inch opening for the thumb, continue seaming to the end. Once seamed, it should resemble another row of knitted stitches.

Weave ends in. Block lightly.

Invisible Seam

With the bound-off edges together, lined up stitch to stitch, insert the tapestry needle under a stitch inside the bound off edge of one side and then under the corresponding stitch on the cast on edge/other side.

BIND OFF EDGE

FOLD ALONG

CAST OFF EDGE

THUMB OPENING

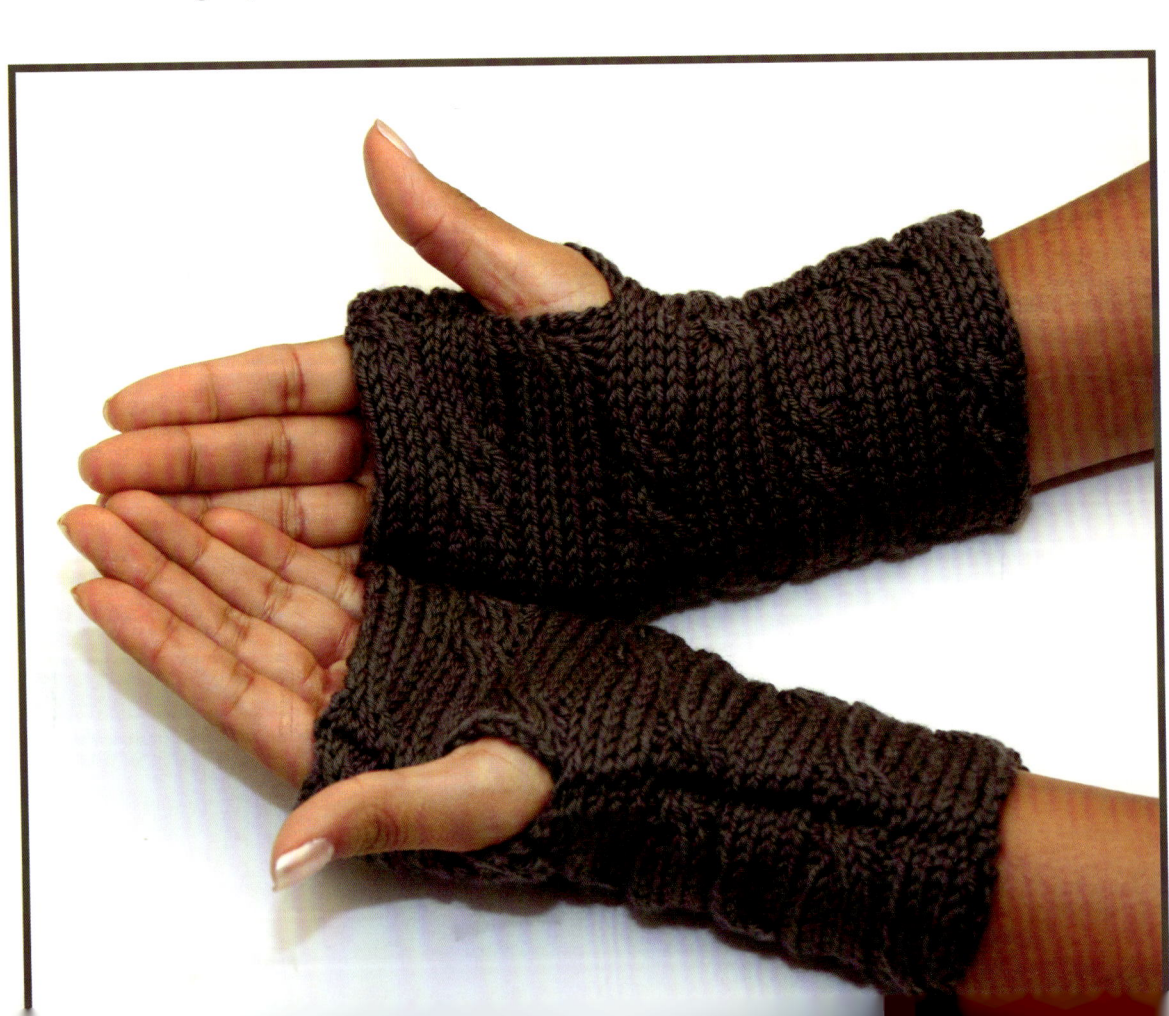

Abbreviations

BO: bind-off

BBO: basic bind-off

CC: contrasting color or accent color yarns

CO: cast-on

CCO: chain cast-on

dec: decrease

dk: double knit

ew: ewrap

GBO: gather bind-off

k: knit stitch

Inc: increase

k2tog: knit two stitches together, right leaning

k2tog-psso: slip 1, k2tog, pass slip stitch over the k2tog

KO: knit off or work the stitch

M1L: make one increase

MC: main color of yarn being used

p: purl stitch

PK: panel knit

p2tog: purl 2 stitches together

pu: pick up

r: row

rep: repeat

rnd(s): round(s)

s1: slip or skip a stitch

sl: slip

sl1: slip a stitch with yarn behind peg

sl1-k2tog-psso: slip one, knit 2 stitches together, pass over slipped stitch

SCC: secondary contrasting color

ssk: slip two stitches and knit them together, left leaning

St: Stockinette st (this can be k or f or u st)

st: stitch (sts) stitches

u: U-stitch

W&T: wrap and turn

wy: working yarn

YO: yarn over

We have made every effort to ensure these instructions are accurate and complete. We cannot, however, be responsible for human error, typographical mistakes, or variations in individual work.

Production Team

Instructional Editor: Pat Novak
Project Editor: Kim Novak
Project Designer: Isela Phelps
Photographers: Kim Novak, Wendell Pace, and Samuel Phelps
Graphic Designer: Felicia Cornish

For more patterns, videos, and looms visit www.knittingboard.com

KB Publishing | ISBN -978-0-9856769-1-9